Stop Shop

Chapter 1: Too Small .... page 2

Chapter 2: New Trainers .... page 11

Chapter 3: One More Shop .... page 17

Chapter 4: Dinosaurs .... page 20

Chapter 5: Quiet .... page 27

Written by Adam and Charlotte Guillain

RISING STARS

Chapter 1: Too Small

Rav was running late for summer club. "Put your trainers on, Rav," called his mum. "This jacket is getting rather small for you, Alpa!" she said.

"Mum, my trainers have shrunk!" yelled Rav, trying to force his feet inside them.

"I think we need to go shopping this afternoon," Mum decided.

Mum and Alpa were waiting for Rav when summer club finished. "It's stopped raining," said Mum, "so let's walk to the shops."

"I want to go on the bus!" wailed Alpa. "My feet hurt!"

"We're going to walk," said Mum firmly.

"It's not fair!" shouted Alpa.

"Stop shouting!" said Rav as people started to stare at Alpa. "Hold our hands and we'll swing you," he suggested to his sister. Alpa stopped yelling and grasped Rav's hand, and soon she was swinging and giggling.

"You'll have to walk now, Alpa," said Rav after a while. "My arm hurts."

"I'm too tired," moaned Alpa. Mum sighed and glanced over at a cafe.

"How about we stop for a drink and a snack before we go shopping?" she suggested.

"Yes please!" said Rav, gazing at the cakes through the window. Mum pushed open the door, the bell tinkled, and they went inside.

They gazed around the busy cafe and a waitress bustled over to them. "Sorry, all our tables are full at the moment," she told them. "You could come back in about twenty minutes."

Mum sighed. "Thanks," she said, "but we should continue with our shopping. Come on, kids."

"No!" shouted Alpa.

"There's nowhere to sit," Mum explained in a quiet voice.

"I want a snack!" cried Alpa and tears rolled down her cheeks. Everyone in the cafe had stopped talking and was staring at Rav and his family. Rav felt his face burn with heat.

"I've got a banana leftover from lunch in my backpack," Rav whispered to his mum. "Alpa could eat that." He just wanted to get out of the cafe as quickly as possible.

"Thanks, Rav," his mum replied, lifting Alpa up and carrying her out of the cafe.

"Stop shouting, Alpa," muttered Rav.

Rav rummaged in his backpack and pulled out a slightly squashed banana. "Here you are," he said, holding it out for Alpa.

"Yuck, it's squishy," she said, turning her head away.

"I was trying to be nice but I'll eat it then!" he said.

"No!" shouted Alpa. She grabbed the banana.

"Open it!" she yelled. Rav peeled the banana before she shouted any more. Alpa was suddenly quiet as she munched on the banana.

Mum ruffled Rav's hair. "Thanks, Rav," she said with a tired smile. Mum pointed at the shoe shop and said "Let's get your new trainers."

Chapter 2: New Trainers

Rav looked at the rows and rows of trainers.

"Which ones do you like?" asked Mum.

Rav was trying to decide between a white pair and a blue pair when Alpa pushed the empty banana skin into his hand. "Ugh!" he said. "Put it in the rubbish bin, Alpa."

"You put it in the bin!" she shouted.

"Please stop shouting," said Rav as he scanned around for a bin.

"No!" she screamed.

Mum took the banana skin and shoved it in her bag.
"Please can we try these on?" she asked the assistant, grabbing the blue pair of trainers.

Rav sat down to have his feet measured.

"My turn, my turn!" shouted Alpa as the shop assistant disappeared to fetch a pair of trainers in Rav's size.

"I've got a little sister, too," he told Rav when he returned. "Just try to ignore her!"

Rav fastened the trainers and walked up and down.

"Do they fit?" asked Mum. Rav nodded. "Great, we'll take them," said Mum, hurrying across to pay. Rav bent down to take the trainers off. "No, keep them on and let's get out of here!" said Mum.

When they were out in the street again, Mum closed her eyes and let out a long, deep breath. "Let's get your new coat another day, Alpa," she said. "I think you might be too exhausted for shopping."

Alpa stared at Mum, then she screwed up her face and burst into tears.

"Okay, Alpa, but you must not cry any more," Mum told her.

Alpa stopped crying and Rav rolled his eyes.

"That jacket really is too small for her," Mum said to Rav. "Come on – one more shop." They headed into the big department store on the corner.

Chapter 3: One More Shop

"We need to go upstairs to the children's department," said Mum, leading them to the escalator.

"This is fun," squealed Alpa. "Let's go up and down and up and down!"

"We can go down in a minute, but now let's find you a nice new jacket," said Mum.

I want to go down now!

"Ooh, have you seen these puppies?" said Mum, trying to distract Alpa. They looked at the multicoloured toy dogs yapping and wagging their tails.

"Can I have one?" asked Alpa.

"No, Alpa, we're getting you a coat," said Mum as Alpa began to wail.

"Oh no!" said Rav. He was getting a pounding headache.

"Could I look at the toys while you choose a coat?" asked Rav quickly.

"Stay where I can see you," said Mum, and Rav hurried away.

An old lady was glancing over at Rav's shouting sister. "What a lot of noise!" she said as Rav scuttled behind the jigsaw puzzles.

Chapter 4: Dinosaurs

Rav watched his mum taking Alpa to the other side of the shop, but he could still hear his sister complaining. "Stop shouting!" he muttered. Then he turned and grinned when he spotted a toy racetrack with shiny cars zooming around it.

Rav examined all the racing cars and decided the red one was his favourite. Next, he looked at some activity books and then studied some boxes of model aeroplanes.

Suddenly, a little but very loud voice shouted, "No!"

"Stop shouting, Alpa!" said Rav, turning the corner …

… but it wasn't his sister, it was a small boy, who looked up at Rav with eyes like ping-pong balls.

"Oops, you're not Alpa!" said Rav. Rav glanced around for the boy's parents and spotted a man peering at action figures.

"I want to go home!" the boy yelled.

Without thinking, Rav picked up a model T-rex and a Triceratops. *"ROAR!"* he bellowed, kneeling down and moving the dinosaurs across the floor. "Once upon a time, two noisy dinosaurs lived in the swamp!" Rav began. The boy stood completely still and tilted his head on one side to watch.

"The two noisy dinosaurs roared all day long!" Rav continued as the boy sat down and kept watching. "One day, the other dinosaurs decided they'd had enough of the noise," said Rav, grabbing a Stegosaurus and a Diplodocus. "They had a meeting to decide what to do."

Rav looked up to see if the boy was still watching and he gasped – now he had an audience!

"Please don't stop!" whispered the little boy's dad. "This is the quietest he's been all afternoon!"

"Yes!" said a woman with a little girl in front of her. "Keep going!"

Rav grinned.

"The dinosaurs decided to have a competition to see who could stay quiet the longest," Rav continued. "Suddenly, the swamp was completely silent." He smiled at the silent children. "They stayed quiet for the whole afternoon," he told them.

"RAV!" came a sudden, familiar yell.

"Oh no," muttered Rav.

Chapter 5: Quiet

Alpa came running across. She stopped, staring at the children and then at Rav. "Oh no, she's going to start shouting again," Rav thought.

There was a pause. Then Alpa's face lit up in a wide grin. "That's my brother," she said, and plonked herself down to listen to the story.

"And the dinosaurs never roared so loudly again," finished Rav, with a beam.

Everyone clapped and cheered – they had loved Rav's story. None of them were shouting any more – they were all smiling!

"Thank you so much!" said the shop assistant. "Please take a dinosaur home with you!"

Wow! Thanks!

"My teacher wants us to collect six things to remember the summer holidays, and this dinosaur is perfect!"

Rav, Alpa and Mum left the shop and headed home. "Let's play that dinosaur game and see who can keep quiet the longest," said Alpa.

What an excellent idea!

Stop Shouting!

What other things will the Comet Street Kids collect for their holiday challenge? Read the other books in this band to find out!

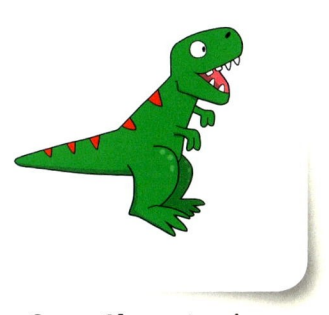

Stop Shouting!

Stranded Panda

A Midsummer Night's Disaster

The Missing Cat

Moonquake

Brilliant Braille

Talk about the story

Answer the questions:

1 Why did Rav feel 'his face burn with heat' on page 7?
2 What did Rav offer to his sister to eat?
3 What does the word 'department' mean? (page 16) Can you use it in a sentence of your own?
4 When Alpa's mum tried to distract her, which toys did she point to?
5 What did Rav pick up in the shop to help tell his story?
6 Why did the parents of the children want Rav to 'keep going' on page 25?
7 Can you describe in your own words how Rav helped in the story?
8 Have you ever helped out with a younger child? What did you do?

Can you retell the story in your own words?